MY FIRST BOOK

SWITZERLAND

ALL ABOUT SWITZERLAND FOR KIDS

GLOBED
CHILDREN BOOKS

Interior and cover Design: Daniel Day

Editor: Margaret Bam

For My Sons, Daniel, David and Jude

Basel, Switzerland

Switzerland

Switzerland is a **country**.

A country is land that is controlled by a **single government**. Countries are also called **nations, states, or nation-states**.

Countries can be **different sizes**. Some countries are big and others are small.

Lungern, Switzerland

Where Is Switzerland?

Switzerland is located in the continent of Europe.

A continent is **a massive area of land that is separated from others by water or other natural features.**

Switzerland is situated in the western part of Europe.

Bern, Switzerland

Capital

The capital of Switzerland is Bern.

Bern is located in the **western-central part** of the country.

Bern is the largest city in Switzerland.

Pilatus, Switzerland

Cantons

Switzerland is a country that is made up of 26 cantons.

The cantons of Switzerland are as follows:

Zürich, Bern, Luzern, Uri, Schwyz, Unterwalden, Glarus, Zug, Freiburg, Solothurn, Basel, Schaffhausen, Appenzell, Sankt Gallen, Graubünden, Aargau, Thurgau, Ticino, Vaud, Valais, Neuchâtel, Genève and Jura.

Population

Switzerland has population of around **8.8 million people** making it the 101th most populated country in the world and the 21st most populated country in Europe.

Lucerne, Switzerland

Size

Switzerland is **41,284 square kilometres** making it the 31st largest country in Europe by area.

Switzerland is the 135th largest country in the world.

Languages

The official languages of Switzerland are **German, French, Italian and Romansh**. German is the most widely spoken language in Switzerland.

In 2014, it was found that almost two-thirds population spoke more than one language regularly.

Here are a few German phrases
- **Guten Morgen** - Good morning
- **Mein Name ist Mondly** - My name is Mondly

Rhine Falls

Attractions

There are lots of interesting places to see in Switzerland.

Some beautiful places to visit in Switzerland are

- **Rhine Falls**
- **Chillon Castle**
- **Chapel Bridge**
- **Matterhorn**
- **Zürich**
- **The Geneva Water Fountain**

History of Switzerland

People have lived in Switzerland for a very long time, in fact the oldest traces of hominid existence in Switzerland dates ba to about 150,000 years ago.

Present day Switzerland was established in the Late Middle Ages originating from the Old Swiss Confederacy following a series of military successes against Austria and Burgundy.

Swiss independence from the Holy Roman Empire was formally recognised in 1648.

Houses at Lauterbrunnen, Switzerland

Customs in Switzerland

Switzerland has many fascinating customs and traditions.

- Each year on the first week of December, a speech is given by St Nicholas, the city's patron saint and protector of children. In the speech, the speaker looks back on the events of the past year.
- Many Swiss people enjoy playing a game of Hornussen. This game is a mixture of golf and baseball and involves two teams and a Nouss.

Swiss Alphorn Blowers near The Matterhorn

Music of Switzerland

There are many different music genres in Switzerland such as **Swiss folk music, metal and electronica.**

Some notable Swiss musicians include
- **DJ BoBo**
- **Urs Bühler**
- **Jojo Mayer**
- **Tina Turner**
- **Mike Candys**
- **Patrick Moraz**

Steak and Rösti

Food of Switzerland

Switzerland is known for having delicious, flavoursome and rich dishes.

The national dish of Switzerland is **Rösti** which is a pan-fried, golden potato patties with onion and sage.

Food of Switzerland

Some popular dishes in Switzerland include

- Fondue
- Tarts and Quiches
- Landjager
- Älplermagronen (Alpine Macaroni)
- Raclette

Zermatt, Switzerland

Weather in Switzerland

Switzerland has a **temperate climate** characterised by moderate summers and moderate winters.

The coldest months in December are **December to February.**

Animals in the park of Peter and Paul in Switzerland

Animals of Switzerland

There are many wonderful animals in Switzerland.

Here are some animals that live in Switzerland

- **Alpine Marmot**
- **Alpine Ibex**
- **Brown Bear**
- **Chamois**
- **Mountain Hare**
- **Bearded Vulture**

The Matterhorn

Mountains

There are many beautiful mountains in Switzerland which is one of the reasons why so many people visit this beautiful country every year.

Here are some of Switzerland's mountains

- **The Matterhorn**
- **Gornergrat**
- **Mount Titlis**
- **Harder Kulm**
- **Uetliberg Mountain**

Switzerland football fan

Sports of Switzerland

Sports play an integral part in Swiss culture. The most popular sport is **Football.**

Here are some of famous sportspeople from Switzerland

- **Roger Federer – Tennis**
- **Fabian Cancellara – Cycling**
- **Martina Hingis – Tennis**
- **Johan Djourou – Football**

Albert Einstein

Famous

Many successful people hail from Switzerland.

Here are some notable Swiss figures

- **Carl Jung - Psychiatrist**
- **Alberto Giacometti - Sculptor**
- **Albert Einstein - Physicist**
- **Jean-Jacques Rousseau - Writer**

Bern, Switzerland

Something Extra...

As a little something extra, we are going to share some lesser known facts about Switzerland.

- **Switzerland has the highest mountains in Europe.**
- **The Alps make up around 60% of Switzerland.**

Swiss Alps

Words From the Author

We hope that you enjoyed learning about the wonderful country of Switzerland.

Switzerland is a country rich in culture and beauty, with lots of wonderful places to visit and people to meet.

We hope you continue to learn more about this wonderful nation. If you enjoyed this book, consider leaving a review!

With Love

Printed in Great Britain
by Amazon